Writers of Wales

EDITORS

MEIC STEPHENS   R. BRINLEY JONES

ALUN LLYWELYN-WILLIAMS

1913-1988

(Photograph reproduced by kind permission of the Welsh Arts Council)

Elwyn Evans

ALUN
LLYWELYN-
WILLIAMS

*University of Wales Press
on behalf of the Welsh Arts Council*

1991

I

P oct, critic, infantry officer, professional broadcaster, university teacher—Alun Llywelyn-Williams had been all of these things and more when he died in 1988. There were many apparent incongruities in his career, notably the fact that this master of the Welsh tongue had grown up in Anglicized Cardiff. But when you met him, as I did at intervals for over fifty years (he was a constant friend), everything somehow fell into place. You might not understand him but you felt that everything was as it should be.

Llywelyn-Williams carried around a special kind of stillness, an air of pleasant but determined reserve, which, very much against his will, could set him apart from those who liked and admired him most. It was when he took up the pen that he let down the barriers. MABINOGI, the first part of an *autobiographical fragment* that appeared in the mid-seventies, is a captivating evocation of his boyhood, into which he weaves with almost novelistic skill an account of the influences and unexpected events which finally made a literary-minded sixth-former who had lived and thought in English dedicate himself to Welsh.

He was born in Cardiff on 27 August 1913. The

1

city was then a place of roaring prosperity, thanks
to the export of coal, and it remained prosperous
when the Valleys languished into depression. In
Alun's boyhood and youth there was little to
suggest that it might become the capital of Wales:
its ethos, as I can testify, was in many respects
English-provincial, even though there was plenty
of activity in the Welsh chapels. Welsh was
seldom heard in the streets, except on Saturday
afternoons when the miners and their wives
came to town.

Llywelyn-Williams's own background, he tells
us, was modestly affluent. After the First World
War the family occupied a large house in Ninian
Road, with a garden at the back where the boy
Alun tried to find enough room to play cricket.
His father was a doctor and a senior civil servant
—the permanent medical member of the Welsh
Board of Health. Dr Llywelyn-Williams must have
been a remarkable man. The son of an ill-paid
country minister in north Wales, he had worked
extremely hard to establish himself in his pro-
fession. When war broke out in 1914 he was forty-
four, but he volunteered for the Royal Army
Medical Corps and went on to win the Military
Cross together with various French decorations.
He was a convinced Calvinistic Methodist and a
staunch Welshman. But he lived for medicine.
Indeed, the whole family, apart from Alun, was
medically orientated. His mother had been a
nurse, his sister became a nurse, and his brother
a doctor. At home, medicine was the main subject of conversation and Alun, the youngest
child, was completely unbothered by *colourful and
detailed discussion of the human body's manifold disorders,*

2

and the methods of treating them with drugs or the knife.
Unprepared visitors reacted differently.

As a boy Alun did not see as much as he might
have done of his brother and sister because they
had been sent, for some reason, to boarding-
schools. Whatever his parents might have intended, he himself had to stay at home, for, as
he says, *it was found when I was four that there was something wrong with the bone of one hand; it had to be kept in a
splint for years.* Not until he was eight did he go to
school regularly. At first he attended a small
establishment run in a private house by two
ladies, where he enjoyed himself but did not
learn much; then it was Roath Park Council
School—a tremendous liberation—and finally
Cardiff High School, whose reputation was at its
peak.

Dr Llywelyn-Williams, we are told, was an indul-
gent father, but *he could be obstinately high-principled*
on such matters as the need to be present at all
the services of Crwys Road Welsh Calvinistic
Methodist Chapel. Alun's mother *was a gentler
character, a calmer personality.* She adored her husband
but found it hard to match his keen appreciation
of public religious exercises. *It was remarkable how
often she was kept away by a headache or a sudden slight cold,
so that we children had to make our way to chapel without
her, feeling secretly envious of her indisposition.* When
Alun's brother and sister were away he often had
to sit in chapel by himself (for his father was
among the elders around the pulpit). The boy's
Welsh being rudimentary he had very little idea
of what the minister was talking about, so he

3

used to pass the time looking at cigarette cards, kindly handed to him by a lady in the next pew.

One cannot but be touched by the description we are given of Dr Llywelyn-Williams's desperate efforts to keep his children Welsh-speaking. Apart from compulsory chapel *he tried out a variety of stratagems. On occasion he would announce that no one was to speak a word of English at meals for the whole day, on pain of a halfpenny fine for every slip into the forbidden tongue.* In Alun's case it was laid down that he must attend the Welsh lessons offered by Roath Park School and take Welsh as a subject (a pretty unfashionable one) in the High School. Alun could not see the point, and Dr Llywelyn-Williams never got round, apparently, to explaining what it was.

At the High School Alun was a useful games-player but by no means a philistine. His eyes were opening to the harsh vigour and frequent beauty of the city, which he and his friends used to wander through from the splendid parks down to the docks, where they would watch the ships being loaded and unloaded. He was reading a lot as well—Kipling, Quiller-Couch and Conrad. Soon his English master had plunged him into the new poetry of T. S. Eliot and Edith Sitwell. Then, encouraged by his sister, he started writing himself. Before long he was determined to be an author—with luck, a poet. In English of course.

There were intimations, though, that there might be more to Welsh than he had thought. A first hint had come when he was quite a small boy. A beautiful young woman, half-Irish, half-

4

Austrian, and devoutly Roman Catholic, who was trying unsuccessfully to recover from a long illness, used to talk to him and read to him. She had a copy of Lady Charlotte Guest's translation of the Mabinogion, and they worked through the stories together. Alun never forgot his introduction to the Four Books by *this dear, fascinating girl*.

Other intimations were more direct. For several years Dr Llywelyn-Williams used to take his family for a month's summer holiday to Pwllglas, a village in the Vale of Clwyd. The journey by slow train, the ride to their lodgings by pony and trap, the games and expeditions in which local and visiting children joined—all these are spellbindingly described in Alun's autobiography. It was in Pwll-glas that Alun really took in the fact that perfectly ordinary people spoke Welsh all day long, not just now and again because they had to. His own Welsh began to improve. And it was near Pwll-glas, during a memorable evening walk, that he first heard of Emrys ap Iwan, who has influenced so many generations of Welsh nationalists.

For the time being, though, the values of Cardiff High School remained in the ascendant. In due course he did manage a pass in Welsh at the School Certificate stage, but it was not much of an achievement. In those days two different papers were set, one intended for candidates who spoke the language at home, the other for those who had had to learn it from scratch. Inevitably they became known as Hard Welsh and Easy Welsh. What Alun got through was Easy Welsh.

5

And he was keen to abandon even that as soon as he got into the Sixth, where he proposed to study his two favourite subjects, History and English, together with either French or Latin.

But now Dr Llywelyn-Williams took a hand in the matter, insisting that the third subject should be Welsh. Father and son had a furious row. No one from the school had ever taken Welsh for Higher Certificate before, and Alun explained that it would be impossible to revamp the time-table to suit one boy. His father was unmoved, and went to see the headmaster. The head supported Alun. What was the point of Alun's taking Welsh if (a) he did not want to and (b) he hoped to try for an Oxford scholarship? Dr Llywelyn-Williams was doubly unmoved. At this stage the senior history master, who knew Welsh very well, intervened. He was prepared to lend a hand with the one-to-one tuition in Welsh that would be required, giving up some of his free periods to do so. This would at least solve the timetabling difficulty. After more argument the offer was accepted, gratefully by the father, most reluctantly by the son—but less reluctantly than might have been the case, since the self-sacrificing master was R. T. Jenkins, no less. Jenkins was on the way to becoming the liveliest university historian in Wales and Alun had the perception to idolize him.

Welsh in the sixth form turned out to be a vast surprise, a surprise which changed Alun permanently. Jenkins and his colleague made him aware for the first time of a body of literature whose best productions, he felt, were fit to stand side by side with the great imaginative creations of the world. *Never*, he says, *shall I forget the set books . . . which worked this miracle in me . . . Reading them was a revelation.* And, adapting lines by T. H. Parry-Williams, Alun closes the first part of his autobiography by saying that during these two years *the Welsh language got her claws into me. I could never escape her again.*

II

Forgetting about Oxbridge, he now aimed at a place in the University of Wales, to read Welsh and then History. Of the four colleges available he chose the one on his own doorstep because the Professor of Welsh was W. J. Gruffydd.

Alun's 'life and opinions' as a student are described in the second part of his autobiography. This, and the third part which takes the story up to 1940, were written some years after MABINOGI and from a different perspective. They lack the magic of that self-contained short masterpiece but offer an interesting account of how his ideas developed. The complete work is called GWANWYN YN Y DDINAS *(Springtime in the City).*

When he entered college, having won a scholarship, he was still determined to be a creative writer—but now in Welsh, or so he hoped. He continued to hanker after History, however, and half-thought it might supply him with his bread and butter. The historical and poetic modes of thinking, as he puts it, fought a continuous battle in his mind.

Alun does not tell us much about the History staff at Cardiff: whether justifiably or not, he did not find them inspiring. But the Welsh Department was different. Gruffydd himself was a formidable figure. Rather like A. E. Housman,

8

whom he despised as a person, Gruffydd combined a tender lyrical gift with a delight in con-
troversy. People used to take his quarterly,
Y LLENOR, not only for the poetry and the articles
but 'to see what Gruffydd had to say this time' in
those editorial notes whose subjects, as often as
not, lay well outside the literary field. During the
Kaiser's War he had served in a mine-sweeper;
afterwards he reacted violently against 'the old
men' who had sent so many younger ones to
horrible deaths. He was a radical and a democrat.
And, like all professors of Welsh in those days, he
was a cradle Welshman who had a superb command of the vernacular. Alun recalls his inciden-
tal oddities—his impatience, his abrupt, untuned
voice—with affection, and his essential greatness
with something like awe. Gruffydd made a very
deep impression on him. This kind of thing hap-
pens often enough, I dare say, when a university
teacher meets an eager and receptive pupil, but
usually the impression wears off. Alun being the
man he was, it did not, or not for a very long
time. Gruffydd's name enters prominently into
his prose, and in due course he composed a noble
elegy to his old master.

Gruffydd and his two colleagues provided their
students with an overview of Welsh literature
from the Dark Ages to the end of the nineteenth
century, and prescribed the study of various key
works. But the main emphasis was linguistic.
Alun had no complaints on that score: a sounder
knowledge of Welsh syntax and a more sensitive
appreciation of the characteristics of the language
were precisely what he was after.

At this point in the story he breaks off to comment on the difficulties of later writers, those of the seventies. In many cases, he says, because Welsh is an acquired language for them, or because the Welsh they were brought up on was so poor, *their linguistic foundations are not as sound as they should be*. But creative writers must have a full command of their medium. If their work is to have the stuff of life in it they must try (rather more ardently than some of them do, it is implied) to gain a thorough grasp of the traditional grammar and to soak themselves in the true native idiom.

That is what Alun did—by steady reading and by attaching himself to any Welsh-speaking students he came across. And he never forgot how difficult it had been. Only a few weeks before his death, when we were discussing his poetry as I prepared to write this essay, he twice asked me to bear in mind the fact that Welsh was not his first language. I found such diffidence both touching and strange, since it is generally agreed that no one of his generation succeeded in writing Welsh that was more correct or more idiomatic. His poems have something of the ancient concision, and in both verse and prose he deploys a vocabulary that enables him, even when he is attacking strictly modern themes, to dispense with English importations and unresonant neologisms. In his literary criticism especially, he gives renewed currency to powerful but half-forgotten words, and turns some familiar ones into terms of art— all with the greatest tact and apparent ease.

It is often said that at some unspecified time Alun

Llywelyn-Williams made a conscious decision to switch languages and become a Welsh rather than an English poet. That, indeed, is the impression one gets from his autobiography, on a cursory reading. But it is hard to see how a genuine poet could have done anything of the kind. Alun makes the point elsewhere that language and feeling, form and content, in poetry cannot be divorced. How was it possible for him, by an act of will, to have bolted the door against one half of his poetic personality? The question comes up in the first volume of YSGRIFAU BEIRNIADOL (*Critical Essays*), edited by J. E. Caerwyn Williams, which includes a recorded conversation between Alun and Bedwyr Lewis Jones. Here Alun explains clearly that no moment of decision ever occurred. The fact is, as he says with engaging simplicity, that having started to write poems in Welsh he *found it natural to go on.*

Even so, there was a residual conflict in his mind. His first book of poems has some stanzas that begin:

> *Deufyd digymod yn ymryson sydd*
> (*Two irreconcilable worlds are contending*).

The verses are unusually obscure: when I asked him about them he told me that they had to do with the continuing clash between the English and Welsh sides of his sensibility. It was a clash that never really ceased. Even at the age of fifty there were still as many emotive words for him in English as in Welsh; this, as he ruefully remarks to Bedwyr Lewis Jones, *must be a weakness in a Welsh-language poet.*

11

But a Welsh-language poet (and a prose-writer who almost always used Welsh) are what he became. Even if there never was a moment of decision, an irreversible choice had somehow or other been made. He often wondered in later life whether it had been the right one (he tells us as much in a 1973 essay) and yet, as he declares in the same essay, it was a choice which he never regretted.

III

The last stanza of 'Two irreconcilable worlds' has a reference to *cynnwrf y cerddi newydd*, the stir of the new poems. These were Audenesque. It is ironical that Alun, having so recently begun writing in Welsh, should promptly bring in a set of English influences.

The most brilliant member of his sixth form, so he writes in GWANWYN, had been a boy from Kent, Raymond Atchison by name (he died suddenly, a few years later). The two were friends, given to taking prodigiously long walks together through the Vale and over the Glamorgan hills, talking literature and politics. They kept in touch after leaving school, and it was chiefly through Atchison that Alun became interested in the poems of W. H. Auden, whose first major collection had recently appeared.

Alun was ripe for such influences. Though he was still entranced by the ancient poetry, and by some of the medieval poetry and prose, that he was studying under Gruffydd, he had begun to feel the remoteness of this literature from twentieth-century concerns. More disturbingly, he was finding that even contemporary writing in Welsh was mostly irrelevant to existence in Cardiff and the towns and villages of industrial south Wales: poets in particular seemed fixated on rural society and, in a restricted and selective sense, nature. The Welsh Romantic movement may have been petering out, but its doctrines, as relentlessly promulgated by Sir John Morris-Jones, still carried weight. Even in 1935, the year Alun left college, he had come across practically nothing in Welsh to match the flood of Anglo-Welsh literature that celebrated the splendours and miseries of life in places like the Rhondda. Alun thought this was a tragic situation, if only because of the effects on the language. He knew that according to the latest census figures there were more speakers of Welsh in proletarian Glamorgan and Monmouthshire than in the whole of Gwynedd, and he believed that if poets and other creative writers used the language to express the intense emotions of devastated communities its future would be secure: if they could not or did not it would eventually die out in the two counties. Alun may or may not have over-estimated the social effects of literature, but in the mid-thirties these were defensible propositions. As he later confessed, the possibility that the language might simply vanish from vast tracts of south Wales in a single generation, which is what actually occurred, never crossed his mind.

When Michael Roberts, impresario of the Auden group, declared that it was time to abandon poetic images drawn from rural life and create 'urban poetry, the poetry of the machine age', the notion tied in perfectly with Alun's thinking. The political attitudes of the group suited him just as well. It was difficult not to be left-wing in the thirties if you were young, had a heart, and lived in south Wales. It was a time of mass unemployment, boarded-up shop windows,

14

dole queues and soup kitchens. Alun, like many of his contemporaries, knew whom to blame:

> *In those aching days we knew who*
> *The enemy was: the greasy bloated capitalists,*
> *The mad politician and the guilty scientist:*
> *It was easy to spot who had caused our cancer and our*
>   *wound.*

The emphasis in GWANWYN being on his development as a person, he does not go into much detail about what was happening in the world. But readers of his early poetry need to remind themselves of the background. In the thirties Fascism and Fascist ideas seemed to be advancing everywhere. Mussolini had been in power for a long time. Hitler was appointed Chancellor when Alun was half-way through college. He had just left college when Italy invaded Ethiopia: the Spanish Civil War began in the following year. Just across the Channel there was *Action Française*, anti-Semitic, anti-democratic, and more papalist than the Pope. In England, as Valentine Cunningham's book BRITISH WRITERS OF THE THIRTIES has impressed on us, prominent authors and artists were proclaiming their love of autocracy, violence and war. The two gurus of English literature, Yeats and Eliot, were making highly ambiguous noises. In Wales, although Saunders Lewis, the charismatic and francophile leader of the young Nationalist Party, denied that he agreed with the political programme of *Action Française*, he combined triumphalist Roman Catholicism with an acrid contempt for twentieth-century democracy. And one or two of his colleagues, Nonconformists though they

15

were, made no bones about their authoritarian sympathies. It was indeed an 'age of anxiety' for young humanists of the Left.

Alun's socialism was at first a matter of theory, but contact with other students and visits to their homes opened his eyes to the realities of life in the industrial valleys. *I saw for the first time the moral rottenness of industrialism, how it had not only defiled the countryside but, as it decayed, brought humiliation and suffering to a whole population.* Not that there was anything wrong with industry and technology in themselves: everything depended on the use made of them. It was society that had to be changed. But how? Certainly not in the way proposed by T. S. Eliot. *However penetrating Eliot's analysis of the appalling state of civilisation, the escape route he suggested was retrograde: it led to a restoration of the authority of the Church and the social values of the past.* Auden and his friends were arguing that the breakdown of capitalism was inevitable, and contending that its destruction would lead to a juster and freer society. For a time at least that was Alun's position also. As his poem 'Remembering the Thirties' has it,

> *We awaited with fear the apocalyptic judgment,*
> *With fear—and with joy. We were born for this.*

He even began calling himself a Marxist—but mainly because it was the trendy thing to do. His attempt to read DAS KAPITAL was a failure.

At one point Alun's newly awakened devotion to the Welsh language and traditional Welsh culture led him to join the college branch of the

nationalist party, *Plaid Genedlaethol Cymru* as it was
then called. This may seem a peculiar step to
have taken, given the contrast between his
socialist principles and the views of Saunders
Lewis. But it should be remembered that *Plaid
Genedlaethol Cymru* was still an organization in the
making, not all of whose members fully agreed
with their leader. However, the official line was
more than Alun could bear, and when he real-
ized that it would not be changed he lost no
time in withdrawing. I ought to add that he
held throughout his life to his belief in self-
government for Wales (and, I think, to his left-of-
centre position). But he never repeated his
incursion into party politics. Even before leaving
college he had come to the conclusion that,
however interested he might be in political ideas,
his mission—the word is his own—was to be a
poet, trying to give voice to human experience
and doing what he could to safeguard permanent
values. In later life he often said that he was a
natural sceptic, temperamentally disinclined to
swallow party dogmas of any kind whatsoever.

Poetry, politics and history by no means ex-
hausted his attention while he was at college.
The most important thing that happened to him
during those years, he says, was meeting and fall-
ing in love with Alis, a red-haired nurse from the
Rhondda. *It had happened before, of course, and it happened again, I must admit. But this was different from any
other time, before or after. He was shaken to the core,*
and it radically changed the character of his
poetry. *Whatever else you need in order to be a poet, I'm
certain that one absolute essential is passionate feeling . . .
Everything I wrote after the agitation of love, however un-*

17

satisfactory, was unutterably better than anything I'd written before. Among his new productions was 'Cefn Cwm Bychan' *(Cwm Bychan Ridge)*, which he submitted to Y LLENOR. Gruffydd accepted it, *not without suggesting a few improvements*, and it duly appeared. This was a kind of accolade. He composed further poems and Gruffydd published these as well.

During his final year Alun took time off to assemble some of his ideas on literature and society into a long essay, 'Barddoniaeth Mewn Oes Ddiwydiannol' *(Poetry in an Industrial Age)*, which also came out in Y LLENOR. It begins with a powerful statement of the need for urban poetry and develops into a reasoned attack on what he calls the Catholic (Roman and Anglo-), élitist, 'classical', 'European' and anti-industrial philosophies of Eliot and Saunders Lewis. Alun's Welsh is still a bit stiff but the article is an astonishing achievement for a boy of twenty.

He was not, as he imagined, quite alone in demanding that Welsh poetry should encompass urban and industrial themes. In retrospect we can see that a move, or, rather, various moves, away from country-based Welsh Romanticism had already begun. And one or two young men of whom Alun was unaware were adopting a stance not dissimilar to his. Nevertheless his article was a landmark, and though not included in his collected criticism it is remembered still. The poet and anthologist Gwynn ap Gwilym quoted from it only recently.

IV

In 1935 the BBC, bowing to sustained pressure, decided to set up a Welsh Region, which would have an all-Welsh programme staff broadcasting in both languages. Alun applied for pretty well every position that was advertised, but without success. However, the Corporation did offer him the vacation job of announcer at the Cardiff studios. He gladly accepted, and he was kept on until the end of September, after which there was nothing for it but to go back to college and 'do research' (in History). But then, out of the blue, came an invitation to work in the National Library of Wales at Aberystwyth. Hastily dropping his research (for which he had not received a grant), he became a librarian in January 1936. On the whole he did not enjoy it, and when, about Whitsun, he was given the opportunity of returning to the BBC, still as a temporary announcer, he accepted the offer without hesitation. Naturally he hoped he would sooner or later be put on the permanent staff, and in a matter of months so he was.

Broadcasting House, Cardiff, was where I first met Alun Llywelyn-Williams. It consisted of two Edwardian villas in Park Place, just across the road from the National Museum. They had been joined together, and extended at the back to provide an orchestral studio: the interior, thanks to the modish tastes of the previous regime, seemed to be all pink walls and art deco furnishings. I

remember Alun as tall and well-built, with a
crop of curly black hair. He had a frank, undis-
sembling look and a pleasant smile; his manner
was composed; he smoked a pipe (unlike the rest
of us, who went in for cigarettes), and we soon
got to know that he was not only a hill-walker
and mountain-climber but also a cricketer. Altogether, now I come to think of it, he was rather
like a John Buchan hero, much though he would
have scorned the comparison.

Quite a few of his new colleagues were not much
older than he was; he fitted in easily and he was
extremely well liked. It was mutual; he recalls in
GWANWYN how exhilarating he found the atmo-
sphere, and in particular how much he gained
from the professional musicians with whom he
worked from day to day. I think we did sometimes wonder, though, why a man whose aca-
demic qualifications were so good should have
opted to become a broadcaster.

On Tuesday afternoons the Torquay Municipal
Orchestra used to contribute from its Pavilion
fastness a ninety-minute programme to the
Regional network. Operationally, the new Welsh
Region remained closely connected with the
West of England, and for some months these
programmes continued to be announced from
Cardiff. The custom was to list the items at the
beginning of the concert and again at the end.
In between, all the announcer had to do was sit
in his office and note down the time each item
took in transmission. It was not a taxing job, and
the average announcer tended to look at a daily
paper or a magazine while the popular overtures

and the musical comedy selections washed over him. So when I walked into the room one Tuesday afternoon it was a surprise to find Alun, pipe in mouth, diligently reading not the WESTERN MAIL or the NEWS CHRONICLE but the DISCOURS DE LA MÉTHODE of Descartes in a new Welsh translation. A trifling incident, but it seemed to symbolize the fact that Alun, though agreeably with us, was not quite of us.

In retrospect some of the reasons why he was so keen to join the BBC are not difficult to understand. Although his tastes were scholarly I do not think he was ever a scholar—he makes the point himself. His primary concern was with literature and the arts, and under Reith the Corporation had a deep respect for the arts and a constant care for standards in the written as well as the spoken word. Again, though we in Cardiff put out plenty of 'light entertainment', we truly felt that the Reithian concept of public service was the foundation of our work—and in our case we were working for Wales.

Alun's colleagues used to look out for his poems in Y LLENOR, but I think we were more interested in the circumstance that he was an editor himself. Towards the end of his college career a few students had got together and resolved to launch a 'little review'. Alun was to be editor, with his friend D. Llewelyn Walters as assistant. The group's objectives were properly ambitious. They wanted to extend the scope of contemporary Welsh literature so as to match the Anglo-Welsh output. They wanted to end the indifference, not to say hostility, which existed between the two sets of writers. They wanted to provide a platform for young artists outside the literary field, and to reflect international trends.

The first number came out in the summer of 1935, and the magazine continued to appear, quarterly, until its existence was abruptly terminated by the Second World War. This was quite a feat for a handful of students and ex-students. No subsidies were available, needless to say. And no contributors were paid—but then no contributors to Welsh magazines in those days ever were. The circulation hovered around the five hundred mark, except in the case of special issues, when it usually went up considerably. Alun and his friends had decided to call their magazine TIR NEWYDD *(New Territory)*. One imagines that the notion came from Alun: he was always a dab hand at inventing titles. (Did he, I wonder, have at the back of his mind Captain Scott's vessel *Terra Nova*, so handsomely commemorated in Cardiff's Roath Park? He must have passed that golden model, and read the name, hundreds of times.)

Considering everything, this pioneering venture succeeded. It carried articles on a whole range of subjects which had been neglected in Welsh—architecture, painting, radio drama and modern music, for instance. Current movements, artistic and intellectual, from surrealism to logical positivism, were noticed. So, of course, was Anglo-Welsh literature. And there was a certain amount of creative writing. But it has to be admitted that the standard of the contributions was uneven, and that the magazine depended more than one

22

would have expected on the goodwill of established authors.

Perhaps the most exciting features of TIR NEWYDD were Alun's own critical essays and his editorial notes, sometimes youthfully pompous but usually well argued. Apart from assailing the National Eisteddfod and the audiences for Welsh plays (who laughed in the wrong places), he concentrated on the themes of his LLENOR article, arousing a good deal of attention in the process. Contemporary poetry in Welsh hardly existed, he wrote; unable to face the urgent problems of the day, Welsh-language poets were locking themselves into either rusticity or the religious glamour of a sham medievalism—or, in the case of Saunders Lewis's brilliant disciple Gwenallt, both. Why, Alun asked, had our poetry always been so backward-looking? One of its most characteristic features was the frequency and duration of its sterile periods, any fresh initiative being regularly succeeded by years and sometimes centuries of imitation and conventionality. In our own time the immemorial life of the remote countryside was disappearing in most parts of the world, and the Welsh language would disappear with it unless our writers speedily adapted to modern conditions.

Alun's first set of editorial notes contains the bold avowal: TIR NEWYDD *believes that an independent Wales should be organised on socialist lines*. Given the conditions of the thirties it was more or less inevitable that the magazine should drift into politics; Alun himself was not inhibited by his renunciation of party from discussing political ideas. What seems remarkable now is that Reith's BBC should have allowed one of its employees to go on editing a magazine whose political attitudes were made so plain. It could only have happened in the Welsh Region, under its first ruler Rhys Hopkin Morris, a former Liberal MP and metropolitan magistrate who had both a passionate regard for freedom of expression and, because of the way he had been appointed, exceptional security of tenure.

Alun made strenuous efforts to alert his readers to the increasing threat posed by Fascism abroad and at home, his campaign culminating in a 'Rhifyn Rhyddid' ('Freedom Number'), which appeared shortly after Munich. As he wrote later, *we tried to strike a powerful blow for reason and for the democratic heritage which was in such danger . . . To define the perils and face them . . . to declare that we stood for the freedom of civilised life and for the radical and Nonconformist tradition of Wales against all forms of reaction—that was our aim.*

Alun was, and continues to be, thought of as, in Welsh terms, a poetic trend-setter. It is strange in a way to find him devoting himself so vigorously to the defence of such Victorian values as reason, understood in a thoroughly pre-Freudian manner. It is an additional paradox that his respect for radical Nonconformist standards was not accompanied by much faith in their doctrinal foundations. The same is true, of course, of his mentor W. J. Gruffydd, who contributed an article to the special number.

After fifty years another difficulty presents itself.

One has to ask how far Alun and his friends (including me) were justified in blithely taking it for granted that socialism was the secular equivalent of twentieth-century Nonconformity's humane vision. After all, we had before us the spectacle of Stalin's terror: should we not have been able to see what socialism could lead to? But the facts were in dispute, and if anyone had managed to prove them we should have said that Stalinist socialism was a perversion of the real thing, as though that disposed of the difficulty. But we were too outraged by the dereliction and unemployment all around us even to consider the possibility that State socialism might be worse. That, at least, is how I recall our mood. Disillusion, so strongly emphasized in Alun's poem 'Remembering the Thirties', came later.

The writers in TIR NEWYDD made fierce attacks on the leaders of Plaid Genedlaethol Cymru. *They defend Fascism at every opportunity, they spit on democratic institutions, they calumniate every attempt to contribute to the only kind of nationalism the Welsh people want, that is, nationalism based on human freedom.* Their practical proposals, too, especially in the economic sphere, were condemned as completely failing to meet the realities of the situation: Alun editorially dismissed them as infantile (*plentynnaidd*). But TIR NEWYDD did not have much use for the Labour Party either. It was not socialist enough, it had no sympathy with the special character of Wales, its party machine was undemocratic, and in south Wales it was tainted with graft. Alun and his friends believed both in Welsh self-government and in democratic socialism of the internationalist kind, and they felt certain that many members of the Welsh Labour Party and *y Blaid Genedlaethol* agreed with them. If that was indeed the case then the two radical wings should get together whether their leaders liked it or not. A group of Bangor students calling themselves *Mudiad y Werin*, the People's Movement, were advocating similar ideas, and TIR NEWYDD promptly gave them its support. (Since Gwyn Thomas, in his short book on Alun Llywelyn-Williams, has mentioned this particular article, I should add that I wrote it myself, under a pseudonym.)

It cannot be said that any of these pronouncements cut much ice at the time, but the attitude of TIR NEWYDD is still of some historical interest, particularly so the sustained critique—the earliest as far as I know—by the democratic Welsh Left of *y Blaid* as it used to be. In the Spring issue of 1936 TIR NEWYDD deplored the establishment of the Bombing School in Llŷn, and after the fire at Penyberth one contributor went out of his way to express his admiration of Saunders Lewis as a person. But there was no change in the magazine's political stance.

V

Alun and Alis were married in the summer of 1938. It was a cheerful occasion, only slightly spoilt by an unexpected incident which occurred before the ceremony. Mansel Thomas, conductor of the BBC Orchestra, was to be the organist. Driving to Crwys Road the moment he got off the air, and anxious not to be late, he was stopped by the police for speeding. When the case subsequently came to court the SOUTH WALES ECHO reported it under a rather neat headline: 'His Tempo Was Too Fast.'

Internationally, the sky continued to darken. Hitler's troops marched into Vienna; Czechoslovakia was abandoned; the Spanish Civil War came to its wretched end; Ribbentrop and Molotov signed their pact; Poland was invaded. Two days later we were at war. Most of us had been expecting it. W. J. Gruffydd's son Dafydd, our drama producer, was already a second lieutenant; the rest of us, that is to say those who were fit and of military age, were waiting to be called up. The Corporation suspended all regional broadcasting; but Mr Hopkin Morris, with typical spirit, insisted that Wales should be a special case. We were to have a daily news bulletin in Welsh; however, it would have to go out from London, where the main newsroom was. So all through the phoney war Alun and a few more of us worked in Portland Place (not always easy to locate in the blackout). We used

to get our information, reams of it, in the form
of teleprinter messages: these had to be sum-
marized, translated, and then broadcast. Our
chief problem was to find Welsh equivalents for
unfamiliar terms, mostly military and economic.
When SPURRELL'S ENGLISH-WELSH DICTIONARY
failed us we had three options: to take over
English words bodily, to extend the meaning of
existing Welsh words, or to invent new ones.
We sometimes had to make up our minds in a
hurry and there was no one to consult—a far cry,
as they say, from the conditions under which
translators work now. It was fortunate that two
of us, Alun himself and Geraint Dyfnallt Owen,
had graduated in Welsh, and were able to keep
us on more or less acceptable linguistic lines.

On 10 May 1940 the false calm ended. Hitler's
armies invaded the Low Countries; soon the
British Expeditionary Force was evacuated from
Dunkirk, and on 8 August the Battle of Britain
began. Then, on 7 September, came the first of
the daylight raids on London and the south-east.
I had been recalled to Cardiff, but the rest of the
unit were still in London—Alis, too. As he was to
write later, Alun had not welcomed the prospect
of joining up *to fight Fascism in defence of a corrupt social
order*, but, faced by the evidence of Nazi Germany's
appalling destructive power, he decided that he
could wait no longer. Alis, who was expecting a
child, went to Alun's parents, now living in Old
Colwyn: he himself went to a recruiting office
near the Euston Road and volunteered for the
Royal Welch Fusiliers (a regiment in which, as
he remarks in GWANWYN, he could do plenty of
walking).

GWANWYN YN Y DDINAS ends thus: *I strolled away, feeling pretty browned off, but still a free man for a while. A new stage in my life was opening up, but after all, whatever lay before me, every experience is grist to the mill of a poet. I was twenty-seven.*

VI

Alun's first book of verse came out in the middle
of the war, a few weeks after the Allies' invasion
of Europe. Not surprisingly, it did not attract
much attention, though Gwenallt gave it a
generous review. It contains the poems he had
written between 1934 and 1942, a year when he
was still in Britain, engaged like thousands of
others in guarding the coast and training for
D-Day. Some of the poems are as moving as any
he ever wrote: others, as recent critics have re-
marked, are prentice-work. He himself said later
that when CERDDI 1934–42 appeared he had not
yet found his own voice, and this is true enough.
One can see, for what the observation is worth,
that he had been influenced by a variety of other
poets, his most obvious debts being to the Auden
group, Eliot (up to a point) and W. J. Gruffydd.

As one might expect, he makes good use of the
industrial and urban vocabulary advocated by
Auden and company. We have references to
mines, slagheaps, neon lights, telephones, wire-
less sets, Triplex glass *(y gwydr triphlyg)* and, very
often, motor cars. Above all, in more senses than
one, we have aeroplanes and the hostile *helmeted
airman*. And there are frontiers. As Cunningham
notes, Auden and his friends, like many contemporaries, were obsessed by Europe and conse-
quently by frontiers: *They perceived frontiers as
running through every department of their lives.* So did
Alun Llywelyn-Williams, except that in his case

y ffin, the frontier or boundary, has a local, Welsh connotation when it is not partly or entirely symbolic.

We must of course beware of *post hoc ergo propter hoc.* Although he repeatedly acknowledges his obligations to Auden and his friends, we cannot assume that whenever he uses their kind of language he is imitating them, since in many respects they themselves were merely reflecting the ideas of the period, as for instance in their fixation on airmen and the air. To say that Llywelyn-Williams was influenced by Auden and company, though true, is not the whole truth: he, like them, was in tune with the time. And this was an achievement in itself, since it has often taken years for Welsh-language writers to catch up with developments elsewhere. His advocacy of urban and industrial themes and his use of the appropriate vocabulary had a revitalizing effect on Welsh poetry, one that is still with us.

As for T. S. Eliot, Llywelyn-Williams simultaneously abhorred many of his ideas and admired his poetic practice. On the stylistic level the young Welshman, like Auden and others, imitates Eliot's trick of bringing things and people on stage unintroduced save by the definite article. Now and again (but only now and again) he experiments with Eliot's 'non-discursive' techniques. And he seems to have taken on board with enthusiasm Eliot's dictum that *poets in our civilisation . . . must be* difficult *. . . The poet must become more . . . allusive, more indirect.* It is true that not every poem in CERDDI and its succeeding volume is 'difficult'—some are transparent enough—but

31

most of them do require close reading. Not until his very last batch of superb poems do we find him frequently going in for what John Wain has called the expression of direct feeling in direct language.

In assessing the influence of W. J. Gruffydd the first striking impression is again stylistic. In modern Welsh an adjective usually follows the noun it qualifies; but the order can be reversed in the interests of rhythm, rhyme, or a sort of instant poeticism. Gruffydd was inordinately fond of this ploy, and the young Llywelyn-Williams uses it frequently. However, this is a surface matter. Gruffydd's influence on the younger man's development ran deeper. Though they were so different in temperament there seems to have been an instinctive affinity between their ways of looking at life and art. In a profile of Gruffydd which Llywelyn-Williams contributed soon after the war to a volume called GWŷR LLÊN (*Men of Letters*), he testifies to the immense appeal which Gruffydd's particular brand of radical Romanticism had for him. And Gruffydd's attitude to some ultimate things must surely have had a bearing on his own standpoint. We learn from the profile that although Gruffydd still bore the marks of his Nonconformist upbringing he had become in effect a secular humanist: in his famous verses to the Llanddeiniolen yew-tree, the grave in Llanddeiniolen *represents the sad ending, the conclusive ending, of a not very sunny existence; it is a grave that offers no hope of resurrection.* And yet for Gruffydd life itself is somehow immortal: *the laughter of 'happy couples' from generation to generation of carefree youth is . . . undimmed by the shade of the yew*. There is an arresting similarity between this and the position that Llywelyn-Williams himself arrived at in his last poems.

The tone of CERDDI 1934–42 is on the whole sombre. According to GWANWYN, anxiety of one kind or another, personal or general, seemed essential to his creativity when he was a young man.

Among the poems composed before the war there are a handful that reflect dereliction in south Wales—but only a handful, which seems curious when one remembers how keen he was to incorporate the concerns of industrial Glamorgan and Monmouthshire into Welsh-language writing. But of course he knew little of those concerns from personal experience. Most Welsh poets of the time had either sprung from the working class, in town or country, or were not far removed from it. Alun Llywelyn-Williams was a bourgeois exception. He ardently sympath-ized with working people, but from the outside. His pre-war address 'To an Unemployed Miner' is an example of the gulf between them: even the spirit of *de haut en bas* is not completely absent. (Nor is it, incidentally, from some of his other work, especially when he confronts the un-educated. One should never forget that he had been brought up a Calvinistic Methodist. He him-self maintained that Calvinistic Methodists were notable among Nonconformists for their sense of hierarchy and for the respect they accorded to learning.)

Another reason why the book contains so few

poems about industrial south Wales is the conviction he soon developed that its troubles and tragedies, however real, had to be put on one side in the face of a threatened universal war. 'Y Byd a'n Blina' (*The World that Troubles Us*), though surprisingly eisteddfodic in manner, forcefully epitomizes what he thought. Wales, he says, has lost her belief in the old teaching that one day there would be a better world; in the mean time her miseries are piling up; but worse things are happening in other countries:

> *Can you also hear today's groans*
> *Along the tender winy acres yonder*
> *And the wild beast's tread on the scorched plains?*

The wild beast (or the wolf—he uses both as symbols of Fascism) can be, and must be, opposed and conquered.

> *The trial will strengthen you: so will the destruction*
> *   that lasts for a time.*
> *Live unconquerably, and the teaching will come true.*

Llywelyn-Williams's public poems, as one might call them, have an intense seriousness and fervour, but no one would claim that they are among the best things in the little book. He is capable of incisive satire, as when he expresses the sheer idiocy of aggressive war in four quatrains that anticipate a well-known scene in Orwell's *1984*:

> *The blind men travel at dawn,*
> *An armed, orderly company, towards the station.*

34

They say war has broken out,
But who our enemies are hasn't been revealed.

We'll be told that in tomorrow's paper ...

And in other poems he throws off telling phrases
like *the sickness that lights/The ready flush of the furnaces*
and *the day of the black, bare, leafless suppliants*. But on
the whole there is too much rhetoric, in the first
person plural, reminiscent not of Auden or
MacNeice but of Stephen Spender. Much the
same is true of the poems in which Llewelyn-
Williams spots the decay of organized religion in
Wales and exhorts his fellow-countrymen to face
the challenge of a presumably secular future.

All these pieces, successful or unsuccessful,
occupy an honourable place in Llywelyn-
Williams's *œuvre*, for it is surely something that at
a time of crisis a young poet should have tried to
speak to his compatriots in prophetic terms.
Shortly before his death I asked him if any of his
contemporaries had done anything similar. No
one, he replied. And what effect had his poems
had when they originally appeared in magazines?
No effect at all, was the answer.

There are a dozen or so non-public poems in
CERDDI. Most of them are love-poems, whose
tone deepens when he and Alis are separated by
his military training for D-Day. Once or twice he
describes the 'rehearsals' for what he presciently
calls *the bitter drama with its botched denouement*. Three
of these non-public poems are particularly striking. 'Wedi Gwrando Cyngor y Meddyg' *(After
Listening to the Doctor's Advice)* is a strange and

powerful lyric: a patient is regaining consciousness in a hospital bedroom; he turns into a
soldier; he realizes that his maps can no longer
be relied on, and he cautiously starts to recon-
noitre a bitterly hostile terrain. 'Cofio Cyfaill'
(*Remembering a Friend*) impresses not only by the
emotional charge it carries—the friend was probably Raymond Atchison—but also by Llywelyn-
Williams's management of tricky metre distantly
related to the elegiac couplet. Finally, there is
'Undod Serch' (*Love's Unity*).

He had already glanced at a subject that would
continue to weigh on his mind, the idea that at
the very root of our personalities we are quite
isolated. 'After Listening to the Doctor's Advice'
ends with this thought. And another lyric,
'Yma'n y Meysydd Tawel' (*Here in the Quiet Fields*),
composed when war seemed imminent, in-
sinuates that even as he and his beloved lie
together,

> *Sudden death whispers, and the heart is alone.*

In 'Love's Unity', however, he declares that the
isolation can be overcome, if only for a moment,
in and by the passion of love. Man and woman
pursue a separate, and a joint, search for the same
explanation (of what? The meaning of life, perhaps). At all events, the passion that unites them
can unite them in every sense. The idea may not
be novel, but it is fearlessly and effectively
communicated.

36

VII

Alun had a rough war. First there was an accident which may seem comic but was in fact very serious. Having been commissioned, he found himself responsible for his company's transport. Taking an official look at the vehicles one day, he managed to fall into the inspection pit: the walls and floor being extremely solid, he injured himself severely—with what long-term effects can only be conjectured. After coming out of hospital he rejoined his regiment and fought in the Low Countries and Germany. On St David's Day 1945 the bren-gun carrier in which he was travelling hit a mine. His driver died instantly; he himself received burns on the face and numerous shrapnel wounds along the right side of his body. However, he recovered sufficiently to return to his duties once more, and he ended his military service in Berlin.

The cluster of poems evoked by the realities of war did not appear in book form until 1956—later still in one case—but it will be convenient to consider them now. The difference between these and his earlier work is extraordinary. What was chiefly missing in CERDDI was a sharp personal vision of the world: too often there were unspecific images, a vague and not very original symbolism. In the war poems he sees things far more concretely: his thoughts grow out of the life, and the death, around him; his language has greater energy and precision. And yet, perhaps because war and the suffering it causes seem always with us, these poems, in spite of their localized settings, have a universal quality which the generalized imagery of the earlier book seldom attained. And, curiously, some of the gloom of that book has disappeared. Altogether, it is as though his determination to be a poet and his years of committed effort have suddenly been rewarded by the muse. Llywelyn-Williams himself put the matter differently in an essay he contributed to ARTISTS IN WALES (1973): *What the war gave me, I suppose, was a salutary direct experience of human suffering and folly of which I had hitherto been a mere passive observer.*

Some of his war poems (there are eleven in all) stand out. 'The Counter-Attack', a loosely structured sonnet, is full of ironic strokes; it also tells us a good deal about its author. When he and his men have disposed of the enemy—

> *After clearing this wood, cautiously reconnoitring*
> *Each innocent hedge and charming glade . . .*
> *After conquering the shattered streets, flattening*
> *What were once neat homes, despoiling their pretty rooms,*
> *After risking the bite of bullets as they dent the walls*

—after all this, when he pauses for a moment and looks at the devastation a harder fight begins. The enemy now is his own instinct of pity,

> *That mean, insidious underminer; against him*
> *Neither tank nor bomb nor gunfire is any use.*

In the next poem Llywelyn-Williams makes his first and only use of the ballad form. 'Baled y

Drychiolaethau' *(The Ballad of the Phantoms)* con-
sists of eight quatrains. It has for its theme a
soldier, still reeling from battle, who turns for
comfort to a woman behind the small bar of *the
last café to stay awake* and discovers that violence
and death have not spared her either: she sees in
her mind's eye, as he sees in his, a butchered
man. Almost every line is dialogue, and this
device somehow enables Llywelyn-Williams to
strip away any trace of sentimentality and give
the incident poignancy of the truest kind.

'Ar Ymweliad' *(On a Visit)* is a narrative poem—
again something he had not given us before.
Novel too is the poem's elaborate organization
—a dozen stanzas of six long rolling lines each,
regularly rhymed *abcabc*. For eleven verses the
first *c* is a trochee and the second a monosyllable:
this is the kind of rhyme one gets in the traditional *cywydd* form (English equivalents would be
'winter, stir' or 'snowing, king'):

> *Daeth heddwch i'w lwyr gyfannu erbyn hyn, mae'n siŵr,*
> *a throi'r tŷ clwyfus yn gartre llawenydd drachefn;*
> *pe gallwn ddychwelyd ryw gyfnos gaeaf*
> *a cherdded eto drwy'r eira mud y lôn ddi-stŵr*
> *i'r man lle bûm, byddai'n dro mewn amser a threfn*
> *newydd, ac nid adwaenwn fyd mor ddieithr â'r haf.*

But in the twelfth verse both cs are monosyllabic,
and the slight change of rhythm is enough to
signal a conclusion. Stylistically, the occasional
archaisms are significant. They connect us with
the most ancient Welsh poetry, which was mostly
about warfare, and they lend a sort of stiff dignity

39

to the diction which is useful in a poem on so emotional a theme.

The first stanza, quoted above, and the next, make it clear that Llywelyn-Williams is writing well after the event and that the narrative is autobiographical:

> Peace, doubtless, must have thoroughly set it to rights by
>   now,
> Turning the wounded house into a home of happiness again;
> If I could go back one wintry evening
> And walk once more through the silent snow along the
>   noiseless lane
> To the place I came to, it would be a change in time
>   and a new
> State of things, and I shouldn't recognize a world as
>   strange as summer.
>
> And perhaps it was only a dream, when I knocked at
>   an arrogant
> Door so long ago: the Baron himself came to open it,
> Staring politely at my uniform:
> 'A, mon capitaine, mille pardons; come in,
>   come in
> Out of this driving snow . . .'

The invitation is thankfully accepted; the Baron shows his visitor the damage done to the château; finally they enter the firelit drawing-room where the Baroness sits alone. The piano is still there, with its books of music, mostly romantic. The visitor makes a would-be polite comment on these; there is a terrible pause, and it emerges that they belonged to the son of the house, recently killed in action. The Baron goes to the piano himself; the music of Chopin and Liszt fills the room, and the sound becomes a kind of communion,

Enfranchising our wounds and freeing our captive hours.

That is all. But the poem abounds in clear-cut images. The château, *a mansion without the magic of age*, leans over a steep valley, made secret by dark pines. Through the glassless windows the east wind bites, spewing snowflakes over carpets, mirrors and chests. The visitor's boots beat out a rhythm on the wooden floors. A crucifix hangs on a wall of the drawing-room, and by the light of the leaping flame the wood shines and pales

As though blood was jerking from the sad intermittent heart.

'Ar Ymweliad' is noteworthy also as perhaps the earliest expression of Llywelyn-Williams's devotion to art (in this case the art of music) as a source of fortitude and happiness in a tragic world.

The months he spent later in occupied Berlin eventually produced three of his finest poems. The central figure is always a woman, and in each instance she is given the name Inge (surely meant to remind us of the Welsh word *ing*, distress or anguish). Inge symbolizes, it would seem, first the suffering that war inflicts on the innocent, then the human love which survives it, and finally the almost unbelievable rebirth of hope.

'Lehrter Bahnhof', a cleverly ordered piece of *vers libre*, shows us a crowd of refugees under the shattered clock of the railway station. Heledd seems to be among them. Princess Heledd is the most heart-rending figure in Welsh mythology, or perhaps history—her brother killed, his palace burnt to the ground (*The hall of Cynddylan is dark tonight*), she herself fated to be a helpless wanderer, the archetype of undeserved adversity. Llywelyn-Williams identifies her with Inge, lying on a heap of rubble and offering her body to the conquering soldiers in exchange for cigarettes or a few bars of chocolate. And he ends by suggesting that the eagle which, in the words of the Dark-Age bard, had been *greedy for the flesh of Cynddylan*, now has his *half-shut eyes* fixed on many another city.

The second of these three Berlin poems, also in *vers libre*, is 'Zehlendorf'. This, we are told in a note, is the name of a suburb from which the Russians mounted their final assault on Berlin. In a public park, under the pine-trees, and near a lake from which children and their boats have long since vanished, we see a shallow grave, marked by a small, anonymous, wooden cross. Inge kneels beside it and kisses the ground. Is it the grave of a coward who fled, of a guerrilla who, like a son of Llywarch the Old, had fought to the last, or of a concentration-camp victim? No matter:

> *The grave has been neatly marked, and above it*
> *The prophetic trees dare not promise*
> *That Spring will visit us again.*

But perhaps it will. The third poem, consisting of five quatrains, takes us to a theatre in the

42

British sector which, though damaged, remains open. 'Theater des Westens' begins:

> It's still raining. Somewhere in the roof
>   The hidden stopped-up mass overflows through the
>   end of a crack,
> And in the confining darkness the wretched regular drops
>   Trickle down and and dirty the loosening carpet.
>
> Oh well, let's look at Inge dancing,
>   Dancing in the concentration of harsh electric light;
> Stronger than the fear that skulks in the pulses of rain
>   Is the music that gives her pliant arms their courage
>
> And directs the joy of every disciplined movement.

As in 'Ar Ymweliad', art seems to purify the suffering that lies all around and to offer some kind of hope. Inge briefly becomes the Olwen of Welsh mythology; flowers spring up where she sets her feet. Even in occupied Berlin *there is a garden to be cultivated* as well as *an infection to be isolated*, and the emotions of the poet and his companions are, for the moment at least, transformed:

> How lightly we ourselves tread the hard stage, and catch at
>   The strength of the sky, the force in the green shoot.

Llywelyn-Williams's war poems have made a lasting impression, as literature and as testimony. The final piece, apart from a rather feeble envoi, is 'Wedi'r Drin' (*After the Conflict*), two stanzas on the theme of leaving Germany:

> Waking is cruel: the dawn so grey
> As it penetrates the dirty windows;

On the bareness of the table, empty glasses
And the shadow of a memory of the uncouth companion
Who netted our sad hilarities in his greedy claws;
Strange parting! Death has retreated.

It would be better if we'd not been allowed to see
The blind cities, the deaf and dumb towns,
The skeleton grin of pretentious houses
Drunkenly dissolved into comic chasms.
We shall hold the picture for ever in the prison of our
    dreams,
The homes of the bowed-down and the walls of the dead.

VIII

Early in 1946 Llywelyn-Williams returned to the BBC. In those days it was fairly common for announcers to become producers, and he was asked to look after 'talks' at Bangor. After some hesitation he agreed—which was pleasant for me since I was to be his Cardiff counterpart. We worked together in great amity, turning out brains trusts, arts magazines, information for farmers, short stories, individual talks and much else. But then in 1948 he obtained a post in the University College of North Wales and resigned from the Corporation. When one remembers how eager he had been to join it the move may seem surprising, but the fact is that during the war the Welsh Region had changed. Hopkin Morris, with others, had departed, and the key positions were now held by youngish people who had not been called up. Prospects for the ex-soldiers were therefore dim, and this may have had something to do with Llywelyn-Williams's decision. But there were other, and probably more important, considerations. He was eight years older now, and he had endured searing experiences: there was in any case an essential gravity about him, and it may be that he was becoming disenchanted by the ephemeral nature of broadcasting. In Cardiff he had enjoyed announcing other people's programmes, but producing them himself was a different matter: most of us have only a limited stock of creativity and I doubt if he liked having to divert so much creative energy from making poems to thinking up ideas for broadcasts. His programmes, as I recall them, were of a high standard, but he was never, so to put it, a natural producer, in the sense of positively enjoying the activity of grooming performers. (In later life he developed an interest in theatre, but again that was a different matter.)

So he became Bangor's Director of Extra-Mural Studies. The prospect must have seemed almost ideal. He would be his own master to a greater extent than ever before; he would be able to communicate to others his love of literature and history, as well as promoting the arts in general; he would be constantly travelling through the mountains and valleys of Gwynedd; his two daughters would continue to live among Welsh-speakers; he could easily keep in touch with friends in the BBC, and he would enjoy the company of scholars (R. T. Jenkins among them) without having to become a full-time scholar himself. In the event he held the position, to the entire satisfaction of the college and his adult groups, until he reached retirement age.

Llywelyn-Williams had lived in Bangor for ten years before his second book of verse appeared. PONT Y CANIEDYDD *(The Singer's Bridge)* contains twenty-six poems in addition to those we have just looked at. There was then a gap of nearly a quarter of a century: Y GOLAU YN Y GWYLL *(Light at Dusk)*, the last volume, came out in 1979. It includes all but one of his previous poems plus nearly two dozen new ones. Eighty-seven poems is the complete tally.

Welsh critics have anatomized this output pretty thoroughly, even deriving from it something like a coherent doctrine of society and life—a philosophy, in the old sense. This way of treating poetry may not commend itself to everyone, and in any case it is noticeable that different critics have reached very different conclusions as to what Llywelyn-Williams's philosophy actually was. Take a subject that for various reasons greatly exercises Welsh literary circles, that of religious belief. One critic has written of *Alun Llywelyn-Williams's quiet, conscientious faith.* Another speaks of *the religious, or semi-religious, undertone* which can be noted in all his poetry. A third asserts that Llywelyn-Williams had no belief of any kind in a transcendent reality and that for him only the power to create works of art offered comfort and consolation. All these viewpoints can be justified by quotations from his poetry—or indeed from his prose, for we find him telling Gwyn Thomas *I have no religious conviction, no faith as such,* while in an essay, admittedly of earlier date, he declares that what Europe needs is *a new vision of man and his place in the purpose of God.*

It would not be difficult to cite other examples of inconsistency. His oft-quoted statement that 'life goes on' *(fe bery bywyd)* is contradicted by his prophecies of nuclear disaster. And so forth. But there is no point in this sort of exercise. Although his cast of mind was meditative and reflective, when he puts on his singing robes what he seeks to produce is not philosophy but poetry—and for the most part lyric poetry, using that term in Bagehot's sense of poems *designed to express . . . some one mood, some single sentiment, some isolated longing*

47

in human nature. Llywelyn-Williams himself wrote that *the poet's aim . . . is to convey or re-create in words a particular state of sensibility, a particular condition of thought or feeling.* He was referring (correctly or incorrectly) to poetry in general, but it is a perfect description of what, in most of his poems, he was trying to do himself. We should go to him, surely, not for a systematic philosophy but for individual insights memorably expressed.

I would guess that over the years Llywelyn-Williams's views, even on matters of the deepest concern, fluctuated, and that he sometimes managed to hold incompatible views simultaneously, as most of us do. In the special case of his attitude to orthodox religion my conjecture would be that quite early on he became a sort of Hardyesque agnostic, *hoping* with varying degrees of confidence that *it might be so.* Towards the end he does seem to have abandoned any belief he still had in a beneficent deity, but the abandonment looks much more like a hunch, born out of physical pain, than an intellectually arrived-at position.

All this is not to say that his poetry has no major themes to which he adhered. Far from it. The public weal, for instance, was never far from his mind. After the war, though, his tone became much more personal, and there was a great deal less in the way of explicit exhortation. What he was keenest on at that time was to give an account of his own psychological make-up: his reflections on Wales, the world, and the human condition are usually made, as the lawyers say, *obiter.*

To anyone who knew Llywelyn-Williams personally, the most surprising poem in the second book must be 'Dechrau'r Daith' *(The Beginning of the Journey)*, which treats life as an evil, or at least a burden to be borne. There had, however, been hints of such an attitude already. It is worth referring once more to his early lyric 'After Listening to the Doctor's Advice'. The convalescent patient in that haunting poem needs all his will-power *to reject the mercy* offered by death. And a post-war meditation, 'Pibau Pan' *(The Pipes of Pan)*, discusses slipping down a rock-face to *marvellous death*, which is a curious expression.

The 'beginning of the journey' is the birth of a child—told in the first person singular:

> *Let there be light, said God:*
> *And at his command heaven was torn from earth*
> *And day from night. Into the bright light*
> *I crawled, blind, naked and alone.*

What is especially moving about this poem is the unambiguous indication that in his youth its author had longed for personal extinction:

> *My first temptation was fear, or the diseased* hiraeth
> *For the paradise of the womb, and primal obliteration . . .*
> *It ensnared me for a long time.*

And it was only conquered by the realization that the intellectual and artistic pleasures of life are unobtainable without its suffering. Once again, the point may not be novel, but it is arrestingly put: the tree of knowledge grows outside the garden of the womb, and it is God who appears

in the form of the serpent, offering *the brave choice
. . . between pain and non-existence.* The expelling angel
is also God:

> *His sword was a flame . . .
> That cauterized the mouth of the paradisal void behind me.*

What was it that made Llywelyn-Williams at
times desire death? (He must have done if he says
so: he was that kind of man and that kind of
poet.) One reason, presumably, was the settled
conviction he had that at the deepest level human
beings are wholly isolated one from another. It
would be easy to point out that such isolation is
a necessary consequence, or merely another
aspect, of human self-consciousness. But of
course the essential loneliness of the human soul
has troubled a great many people for many centuries, and continues to do so. Why it should
have weighed with such devastating heaviness on
Alun Llywelyn-Williams we shall never know.
One tends to look for clues in childhood experiences. Was he sufficiently conscious, as a boy, of
being loved? We learn from GWANWYN that his
mother, though kind and gentle, was a person of
unusual self-restraint. Alun's admired father was
much absorbed in his work and the requirements
of his chapel. Why did parents of their background and period pack two of their children off
to boarding-schools? And what about those years
the boy Alun spent at home, nursing his suspect
arm? They seem to have been solitary enough.
In GWANWYN Alun tells us far more about himself than he was ever likely to do in conversation:
even so, the story is too well-ordered and the
facts seem too carefully selected for this account

of his boyhood to carry total conviction. We are left guessing.

One of his war poems, in which he describes his stay in the ward of a Belgian military hospital, is significant. The patients, he says, talk together; they compare notes about their narrow escapes; they stare out of the windows at the same sky; but the psychological trenches between them are too deep for real communication: in the end every man's memories are his own. A later poem, 'Tydi a Minnau' *(You and I)*, brings his difficulties into focus:

In a conversation, when we utter words, we are alone . . .
The messages come to us pleading
To be received and interpreted . . .
Smoke rises from the priestly pipe
Or the cigarette, and through the wall
The neighbourly piano eructs; we listen attentively
To one another's words, and watch their frail harmony
Weaving like a groping sunbeam across the moor.
What are you saying? And seeking? What are we
    thinking?

It's a bitter captivity, in which we look into the
    provoking mirror,
In which the valves colour up but the signal strength is
    not enough;
The meaning is clear but we know there's a hidden
    meaning,
A secret under the verbal veil, a truth to be reached,
And understood, before the impossible loneliness is
    swept away . . .

Swept away it could be for him, we know, in the

embrace of love. One of his final poems, 'The Road to Abergwesyn', expresses his abiding gratitude to Alis for so often *melting his loneliness into her strength*. But relief from the misery of being separate and apart could also reach him as a sort of divine grace. 'You and I' ends thus:

> *. . . last night we came to a small, narrow lane*
> *Over the last ridges of the world; and the sea*
> *Was before us, smooth, palely grey, and the multitude,*
> *The multitude of lights around the calm estuary;*
> *No one spoke a word: the purple mountain*
> *Said it for us, the hammer-blows*
> *Of unnecessary words were stilled: and in the abundance*
> *Of silence, pregnant like a holy Sunday,*
> *We saw, and fully possessed, the ungainsayable truth.*
> *Come, living quiet, ravish our empty loneliness.*

Llywelyn-Williams is here relating what many would call a religious experience. There is no doubt that he had a Wordsworthian, semi-mystical approach to the natural world, and especially to hills and mountains—an emotion that for a while seemed merely to complement his interest in urban and industrial life but which proved in the end to run far deeper. One of his earliest published pieces, in *vers libre*, describes the hills of Glamorgan as bare stoics, unconcerned with man's anguish, yet still his salvation and purification. 'Ystrad Fellte', a highly-wrought production in the second book, is on the surface only a happy recollection of an expedition to the country with a friend, but it reveals his almost startling affinity with nature—with nature *per se* rather than particular birds or animals or flowers, though he writes about these on occasion. There have always been plenty of good poems about the countryside in Welsh, but those of Llywelyn-Williams, soon counted though they are, have a depth of feeling for the natural order, and a rapport with it, that is quite uncommon.

Such quasi-pantheism may have little to do with the religion they taught him at Crwys Road, but it is closely related to the strain of pure joy he felt from his earliest years in the superficies of the world and in physical activity. He responded to the beauty about him as keenly as any neo-Georgian. In his second book, when his descriptive powers had matured, he gives us some magical vignettes—of wild swans flying into the distance, of a drive through the snow, of a mountain ash, and of the Menai Straits in the evening, with the last beams of the sun, the lights on the opposite bank, and the first stars, all reflected in the water. Equally brilliant are his miniature townscapes—townscapes with figures: June in the city, with children playing in the park, London Airport, with its painful farewells and unruffled pilots, London houses, guarded by rows of milk bottles. The third book, too, has some memorable pictures, this time of bridges and ancient buildings in France and Greece. What these short poems convey is not merely the sense of place but the mood of heightened awareness in which the places were observed. He must still have been at heart the boy who wandered around Cardiff, entranced by what he saw. In their combination of emotion, apt words, insinuating rhythms and flexible rhyme-schemes the poems are virtually untranslatable; readers who know Welsh can only regret that Llywelyn-Williams did not give us more of them.

But his world is to be wrestled with as well as wondered at. Hills and mountains are to be walked over and climbed; the sea is to be sailed on—the four stanzas of 'Pan Oeddwn Fachgen' (*When I Was a Boy*) splendidly recapture the youthful pleasure of handling a small boat. Danger gives it all an extra kick: in 'The Pipes of Pan' he declares that we have an instinctive urge to do battle with the ferocious side of nature as our forefathers did. Some may think, mistakenly, that nature is permanently under our control:

> *The speeding driver on the macadam road*
> *Who steers, carefree, over the open moorland*
> *Doesn't see the shadows of the trees of past centuries*
> *Or the traveller of past days, here on the slopes of*
>   *Y Foel or Y Garn,*
> *Weakened by fear and cold, by the oppression of snow,*
> *Standing on guard, with his last javelin,*
> *Against the cruel patience of the wolf.*

But 'the old adversary' is still lying in wait for us. What is more,

> *We need him, the ancient discipliner,*
> *Animal's challenge, or the naked snow or the destroying*
>   *flood.*
> *And wherever he may be we must search for his*
>   *hiding-place*
> *And demand that combat which is life indeed.*
> *As we climb the rock on which the feet of our cautious*
>   *forefathers*
> *Never ventured,*

Setting our nailed boots on the steep peril,
Clambering from toe-hold to overhang up the rigorous cliff
We feel the thrill we had lost.
And sometimes we find him, the keen, unconquerable
* friend,*
Waiting for us there in the stony place
When the rock breaks away, when our hold fails,
And he comes to embrace us as powerfully as ever
And throw us for sport on to the descent to marvellous
* death.*

The joy of physical activity and the lure of the danger that goes with it are unusual themes in the Welsh poetry of the last century or two. Given the working-class basis of our culture this is not surprising: until recently hill-farmers and their labourers had quite enough physical activity to be going on with, and danger was always present where men cut coal or rolled red-hot steel. Not many poets wanted more of either commodity for its own sake. Llywelyn-Williams's attitude testifies to his privileged urban background.

Although he was not yet forty when his second book of poems appeared, a strain of retrospection runs right through it. The passage of time is a central feature. His strong feeling for history extended to his own personal history: autobiography *was always breaking in*, and the phrase 'emotion recollected in tranquillity' fits much of his poetry exactly.

He thinks of his youth with sadness and delight. 'Pan Oeddwn Fachgen', with its glittering images and dexterity of rhythm, inevitably reminds the reader of Dylan Thomas's 'Fern Hill', composed during the same period: it carries the same kind of remembered wonder and the same consciousness of overmastering time. In Llywelyn-Williams's poem, though, the impression made on the boy continues to influence the man. The warm suns of childhood have set for ever, but

> . . . *the light in the dusk across the bay,*
> *That's what remains*
> *. . . it shines*
> *Still on an uncompleted voyage.*

In 'Y Wers ar y Piano' *(The Piano Lesson)*, his thoughts turn to himself as a young man. As he watches his daughter Eryl feeling her way into the world of music he is greatly moved, for without realizing it she is re-creating one of the charmed evenings when he himself was introduced to those very works by his friend.

The stress on *hiraeth* in these and other poems might suggest sentimentality or mawkishness. But no: he triumphantly escapes them. He was well aware, however, that dwelling excessively on the past was a temptation he had to resist. The idea comes out clearly in a late lyric:

> *Between sleep and waking, at dawn,*
> *The world falls into place only slowly;*
> *It's a struggle between the drugs of night and the*
> *   reality of day.*
>
> *How many rooms, I wonder, have lapped us into sleep?*

And this particular room, which is it?
In every bedroom in the world a dream half comes to life.

The morning light arrives through an unexpected window;
The colour of the carpet, the position of the door, the
*   bare wall,*
They're all unfamiliar; what image can we depend on?

We open our eyes fully; the familiar present
Flows back; and yet the past, how dogged it is,
How comforting to the child who once existed, how
*   dangerous to the living.*

In the title poem of his second book, 135 lines of
vers libre, he considers more generally the passage
of time and our consciousness of it. The poem
has great richness of reference and many layers
of meaning. Pont y Caniedydd itself is a bridge
over a little stream in the Brecon Beacons. A
group of friends are walking the open country,
as they have often done previously: they descend
to the bridge before moving up to the crests,
from which they will be able to see in the distance the industrial town where they live. It soon
becomes apparent that the bridge symbolizes the
junction between the past and the future—of
Wales, and of communities and individuals:

Mae dau dro yn yr hewl, a phlyg annisgwyl
ar i waered tua'r nant;
a dacw'r bont, yn cydio'r ddwylan,
a'r ffrwd yw'r ffin soniarus, cyn dringo
drwy'r bedw a'r cyll at iet y mynydd
a'r llechwedd hir sy'n rhagfynegi'r bwlch.

(There are two curves in the road, and an unexpected fold,
On the way down to the narrow valley.

> *And that's the bridge that connects the two banks.*
> *The stream makes a melodious boundary before we climb*
> *Through the birches and the hazel trees towards the*
>   *mountain gate*
> *And the long rise that prophesies the col.)*

The little party sense that the past is all about them, and it makes them uneasy:

> *We are afraid . . .*
> *Afraid because we feel our lack of a past, or perhaps*
>   *because*
> *An unfamiliar past is always close to us here . . .*
> *We fear every past except the brief one which is our own.*

The old order is represented by a bent figure whose Welsh is an unknown tongue to his sons and daughters; by his talk of a once-flourishing village hereabouts, now abandoned and grown over; by the neighbouring homes of great men like Henry Vaughan and Howell Harris, and by a mansion which the county family no longer occupies. The group do not feel comfortable in its stately apartments:

> *We trespassers from the age of anxiety . . .*
> *A small remnant in torment between two*
> *Cultures, savour the faint fragrance*
> *Of the faded flowers, and try to sense their significance.*
> *To the unpedigreed stranger this is no country of his.*

But the Welsh place-names, so much older than the country house, are more resonant than ever.

In the second section of the poem the group cross the *melodious boundary* and start climbing to-

wards the gap and the distant town, whose all-
too-familiar features are mercilessly delineated.
When they get back, though, all will be seen in
a new light because of their brush with the past.

The closing lines of the poem revive the image
of the junction between past and future, and
confront us, suddenly but effectively, with the
idea of our essential isolation as individuals:

> . . . between the two banks, here in this elect meeting-
>   place,
> This hidden fold in time, perpetual music
> Flows for the man who hears it like healing blood:
> Day speaks to night, and water to fire,—
> Within yourself, solitary pilgrim, is
> The fulfilment the present offers, with its redeeming pain.

'Pont y Caniedydd' is the longest and most
ambitious production in Llywelyn-Williams's
œuvre. Its stylistic obligations to the Eliot of the
'Four Quartets' are clear, but in no way diminish
its value as a reflective poem. It has many inci-
dental felicities and many points of interest,
including the last direct mention of the poet's
experiences in the war. And we meet the airman
again: he is, first, the superman:

> Above us the winged pilot, the shining searcher,
> Smiles at the incredible map of the slow ancient world,
> Its rusty fields and squat churches.

Then he becomes the sinister figure who might
end existence for all of us—the trespassers from
the age of anxiety are also the

Precursors of the final destruction to be wrought by the pilot.

It is evident that Llywelyn-Williams, writing under the shadow of the atomic bomb and *in torment between two cultures*, was uncertain whether Wales and its language—or, come to that, the human race—would survive. A few shorter poems, presumably composed during the same period, make the point with equal starkness.

IX

'Light at Dusk', Llywelyn-Williams's third book of verse, takes its title from the last stanza of 'When I Was a Boy'. Though the number of poems he had composed in the twenty-three years since PONT Y CANIEDYDD is small, some of them represent the peak of his achievement.

Literary tastes had been changing in Wales as in England. When his first work was printed in Y LLENOR there was a great gulf between written and spoken Welsh; furthermore there was still a strong late-Romantic tendency to assume that words and phrases taken from the medieval language would prove an adornment to poems on most subjects. His own earliest poetry contains words like *gnif, anolaith* and *eilchwyl* (though he did not use them for long). Wardour Street Welsh gradually disappeared, and T. H. Parry-Williams had brought a rasping dialectal note into Welsh poetry which Llywelyn-Williams much admired. His own Welsh was basically bookish, but he had lived long enough in Gwynedd to acquire some of its vernacular vigour, and the shorter poems in this third volume are composed in an informal, direct style which is altogether different from most of his previous work.

The joy he feels in the visible world comes to a climax in the short series of European vignettes. But he also considers the approach of old age.

His life was already one of suffering. In the face of the near-certainty of a bleak future his lyrical gift blossoms, and he gives us verses of piercing sadness and beauty.

The title of one poem, 'Diwedd Cyfnod' (*End of an Era*), speaks for all the rest. The thought of mortality, which had always haunted him, is now more pressing: there are no more comforting concealments. 'Y Gaeaf Wrth yr Afon' (*Winter Near the River*) sets the tone. *The clarity of winter* washes *every leafy mercy* from the eyes; Menai, it is implied, has become Jordan. In another lyric, 'Pwy Piau'r Wlad?' (*Who Owns the Country?*), he even surrenders his Welsh hills and mountains to the stranger, the young climber from distant parts, because he, too, loves them in his own way:

> *Every crest, every unobtrusive crevice,*
> *Every ledge, every spare fissure,*
> *He has conquered them and he loves them.*

> *Who am I to grudge this man*
> *His stubborn possession*
> *Of my valley's hidden joy?*

Two lyrics provide metaphors for the passage of time and the advance of age. One is 'Gwerthu'r Dodrefn' (*Selling the Furniture*). In the other, 'Acer o Dir' (*An Acre of Ground*), he surveys the bank at the end of his garden which he had planted with trees. He names them all before reflecting that

> *... time is cunning: the music of May*
> *Turns into leafy abundance, then glowing flame,*
> *then bare branches.*

'End of an Era' puts the matter more plainly:

> *Years ago we used to fear*
> *The destruction of the world*
> *Under showers of steel and a crowd of flames.*
> *But it wasn't quite like that;*
> *Death doesn't always*
> *Operate so slickly.*
>
> *A man decays slowly . . .*
> *It takes time*
> *For our machines to slow down,*
> *For us to notice that letters*
> *Arrive less often*
> *And the papers later in the morning;*
> *That nobody's listening*
> *Or guarding the empty boundary*
> *Between dream and existence;*
> *That there's no one now*
> *Who answers our prayers.*

A couple of poems in the second book had indicated that he was beginning, with great reluctance, to withdraw from his father's religious faith. This poem, like some throw-away lines in others, signals pretty clearly that for him it had now vanished altogether.

He seems to feel also that religion generally, at least in its traditional, rural, Nonconformist form, is finished. 'Bethel', in its three stanzas, symbolizes a great deal. Searching for the old chapel one day, Llywelyn-Williams finds that it has been bypassed. He knows it stood at the top of a hill, but the grand new road runs through the bottom of the valley. Turning the car round, he eventually discovers the track and starts to climb it. But the building he reaches is empty, dilapidated and locked—and there is no one around who can even talk about the people commemorated on the gravestones.

The world is indeed *very evil*. In 'The Lights of the City', which is full of brilliant and (unusually for him) somewhat repulsive images, and in two *vers libre* pieces, he proclaims a new and deep suspicion of modern technology and science. 'Yr Hen Ormes' (*The Ancient Oppression*), a combination of Greek and Welsh mythology, expresses not only his continued loathing of violence and war but a dreadful fear that they may be a necessary part of the human condition.

Many of these darker poems belong to the same period as the vignettes. It would be a mistake to think of Llywelyn-Williams as a constant prey to existential gloom. Even when life became very difficult for him there were respites. One lyric tells of a quick, unexpected kiss his wife gave him as she passed by, and of how it made him feel young and passionate again. Early Spring provides him with a moment of beauty, even of hope. As he goes for the car in the morning he notices the daffodils on the lawn and a blackbird singing its heart out on a bare branch. 'Gwanwyn fel y Daw' (*Spring as it Comes*) continues:

> *. . . the sun pierced suddenly through the nape*
> *Of the dark bush, chose a black leaf*
> *In the midst of pale winter's shadows*
> *And turned it into a shiver of precious light.*

64

What psalm shall I sing over the purr of the car?
Who will listen? There was joy for a time;
It doesn't matter now that the cold wind of March
Is ruffling the flowers, that the bush is dark and the
    bird silent.

There were more permanent encouragements
(to use Cardinal Newman's word). As we have
seen, art in all its forms was for him a strong
support in a difficult world—*light at dusk*. But his
last work suggests that as he grew older what
meant most to him was something more
ordinary and elemental, the golden chain, as he
called it, binding him to wife, family and community. 'The Road to Abergwesyn', which we
have mentioned already, is a longish *vers libre*
address to Alis, in which he contrasts their first
visit to that moorland village a quarter of a century before with a recent one, and thanks her
for what she has been to him in the meantime:
it is a most striking and tender poem. And
among the small crop of late lyrics there are
other unmistakable references to their happiness
together over many years. Desire may be failing,
as he tells us plainly enough, but that is of no
consequence.

Llywelyn-Williams's feeling for the Welsh community, past, present and to come, emerges so
often that there is no need to dwell on it. He
also has the traditional Welsh veneration for ties
of blood. In previous poems he had spoken of
his grandmother, his father and his brother:
now, in a lyric called simply 'Y Teulu' (*The
Family*), he casts a compassionate look at all his
country forebears. And he connects the past of

his clan with its future: the chest that holds the family tree must be handed on safely *to the one who comes next*. These concerns fuse in the final poem, 'Tynyfedw'. In spite of everything, when he looks at his daughter Luned, her husband and their children, who have repossessed part of the Welsh countryside, he dares to hope that life will indeed go on and that the Welsh community and even the Welsh language will endure.

X

Llywelyn-Williams was a self-conscious poet, in the best sense of the adjective. Although his *œuvre* was not large, phrases like *my concern as a poet* and *my work as a poet* flowed readily from his pen, and he was always willing to explain his poetic aims and methods.

At first glance his art seems derivative: some of the influences that bore on it have been mentioned in this essay. But the impression is misleading. The more you study his poetry the more certain you become that beneath his undoubted receptivity to literary fashion he was always, as they say, his own man.

He has been called *bardd y vers libre*, the *vers libre* poet. This is an odd description, for he certainly was not the first to write good *vers libre* in Welsh and he soon ceased to confine himself to that form. On the other hand he tended to use it for his longer poems and he did take the form with great seriousness, as witness the substantial essay he wrote on the subject.

His own use of *vers libre* is individual. For one thing it is strongly rhythmic. He does not hesitate to introduce metrical passages and he has at all times a marked tendency to slide into the iambic pentameter, especially in concluding lines. 'Tydi a Minnau' begins metrically, moves off into *vers libre*, and returns to metre. En route are encountered straightforward iambic pentameters, blank verse of a freer kind, individual unmetrical lines, a hexameter and an alexandrine. One might call it, I suppose, irregular *vers libre*. The remarkable thing is that it all comes off so well.

Many of Llywelyn-Williams's metrical poems are just as irregular, in a different way. To reverse Johnson's remark, they stand the trial of the ear better than of the finger. In some poems, even short descriptive pieces, slight things with no particular depth of thought, not only does the number of syllables in corresponding lines vary extraordinarily; the number of beats, or pulses, does so as well. And yet the fluctuations once again seem inevitable and right. It is hardly going too far to say that Llywelyn-Williams's *vers libre* approximates to metre and his metrical poems approach free verse. In either case his primary object is to adjust his lines to the rhythm of the spoken word. His autobiography and some of his essays make this clear, and during our last conversation he confirmed that it was so.

His use of rhyme is as distinctive as his prosody, but not, it might be thought, as effective. When he writes in metre he can set up rhyming patterns of great complexity and beauty and maintain them to the end, but he is capable on occasion of taking some quite elementary scheme and altering it as he goes along, with slightly disconcerting results. In his *vers libre* he often uses rhyme, conventionally enough, to mark off paragraphs or signal a conclusion, but here again the rhyming can appear arbitrary. Out of 135 lines in 'Pont y Caniedydd', for example, thirty-five are either

rhymed or assonanted. Fourteen of the rhymes
come at the end, arranged as in a Shakespearean
sonnet. The remaining twenty-one are scattered
here and there, with clumps of unrhymed lines
in between. The motivation is hard to fathom.
All one can be sure of is that such a careful crafts-
man could not have been acting on caprice, for
no poet of our time thought of his work more
consistently in terms of its sound.

Musicality is indeed an outstanding feature of his
poetry. (The few years he spent as a BBC announcer were, according to him, what first gave
him a genuine awareness of music, making him
realize in turn the importance of the musical
component in his own art.) Some of his lines
positively sing their way into the memory:

> *Rhwng cwsg ac effro, yn y bore bach*

for example, and

> *Mehefin sydd drist yn y dro*

and

> *Byth ni ddistawan, adleisiau'r nosau cân.*

Oddly enough, the only sort of verbal music that
made no appeal to him was *cynghanedd*, the traditional Welsh system of alliteration and internal
rhyming. He did try his hand at it once or twice,
but half-heartedly, and his essays indicate that
for him *cynghanedd* was no more than a set of
mechanical rules which made poets worry more
about sound than sense. He never really accepted

the idea that, the rules of *cynghanedd* once mastered, people could think and feel in it, so that the question of sacrificing sense to sound no longer arose. Most literate Welsh people are drawn almost instinctively to the 'strict metres' even if the finer points are beyond them; in this respect at least Llywelyn-Williams was what he sometimes feared he might be, an Englishman writing in Welsh.

To revert to his *vers libre*; he was, as he stated more than once, well aware of its inherent dangers, especially its tendency to turn into disguised or glorified prose. But one cannot say he entirely avoids them. Meditative, reflective poetry (and quite a lot of his *vers libre* falls into this category) is in any case notoriously hard to keep on the emotional boil.

In the conversation with Bedwyr Lewis Jones reproduced in YSGRIFAU BEIRNIADOL he said that every poem he had ever written had emanated from some definite experience or other; but among those experiences he included vague feelings, thoughts that had struck him, and reactions to hearing music performed. The experience would be followed by two periods: first, weeks or months during which nothing much seemed to happen, and then a prolonged struggle to get the experience into words, the thing becoming more complex the more he chewed it over. Such at least was the usual process, though, as he explained to Gwyn Thomas in another recorded interview, it could be short-circuited. Nothing could be more different from the methods of his contemporary, Dylan Thomas (*I make one image*

... *let it breed another, let that image contradict the first,* and so on). In the case of Llywelyn-Williams it looks as though on occasion he began with general ideas and constructed the images later. If so, it might account for the shortage of original metaphors and similes which one sometimes notices in his ruminative *vers libre* pieces.

In the end it is the intense feeling in his poetry that matters—that and the impression he always gives of a stunning and admirable veracity. After reading his poems we are convinced that here is a brave and sensitive man telling us the truth—not every intimate fact but the truth—about himself and his view of the world. Unlike many Romantic poets, he wears no masks. As we have recognized, by and large all his poetry is auto-biographical, and, whatever may be the surface changes in his work, his major characteristics—his deep pessimism, wonderfully combined with joy in life and in physical activity, his reverence for nature and love, family and community, his compassion and magnanimity, his devotion to the land and language of Wales—these and others shine through from first to last; they are rock-like.

XI

When Llywelyn-Williams joined the college staff at Bangor he presumably thought it would be appropriate for him to obtain an MA degree. This meant a thesis. The subject he chose was that Romantic movement in poetry with which W. J. Gruffydd had been prominently associated. The dissertation was completed by 1957 and published three years later. But before then he had produced a very different kind of book, a contribution to a new series called CRWYDRO CYMRU (*Wandering Through Wales*). Llywelyn-Williams was responsible for the volume on Arfon, the ancient division of Gwynedd, including Snowdonia, which he had been getting to know for twelve years. In 1964 he contributed the volume on Breconshire, which he had so often explored as a young hill-climber and where he had been stationed during the war.

These are rich books, born out of affection and keen observation. His aptitude for descriptive writing has full scope, whether he hits off a scene in a phrase or puts together an elaborate set-piece. Quite rightly, he gives us plenty of facts, but these are irrigated by a stream of pleasant reminiscences. He is unexpectedly knowledgeable about architecture: churches and castles make their appearance, of course, but so do noteworthy pubs and cottages; we learn a great deal about local building materials. Every page has its quota of literary and historical allusions, for to him the past was all around, waiting to be recognized and identified. Yet these are more than guidebooks. He has a sociological eye, and his remarks on the changes going on in Welsh society, nationally as well as locally, are likely to have permanent documentary value. The style of both books is upbeat, but the reader is always conscious of his concern for the Welsh community and the Welsh language. Among the most poignant passages in either book is the account he gives of meeting a blind old man who was the very last person who could speak Welsh in the Breconshire village of Cwm-du.

Naturally enough, the book Llywelyn-Williams based on his thesis is more austere in style, though the title, Y NOS, Y NIWL A'R YNYS (*Night, Mist and the Island*), might lead one to expect otherwise. It is primarily a study of the favourite symbols and themes of the Welsh Romantics, against a backdrop of earlier movements in Europe and England and of social changes in Wales itself. He provides a wide-ranging and penetrating survey, stylishly distinguishing and evaluating the threads that made up the Welsh pattern.

A remarkable aspect of the book is its conclusion. In the final chapter Llywelyn-Williams seems to recoil from the praise he has been heaping on various elements in the movement, and to cast doubt on the validity of Romantic poetry generally, recovering himself only in the penultimate paragraph, which emphasizes that Romanticism equipped Welsh literature with a new kind of sensibility. However respectable his reasoning, it

73

is hard not to suspect that after devoting so much time and energy to Morris-Jones, Gwynn Jones, Gruffydd and the rest, he had grown rather tired of them all.

Back in 1948 Gruffydd's poetry in particular had evoked his almost unqualified admiration. In the profile published in that year he showed that although Gruffydd was unquestionably a Romantic poet—indeed the only member of the movement who had never changed his position —his Romanticism was not of the conventional kind. Unlike Morris-Jones with his antiquated division of themes into poetic and unpoetic, Gruffydd held that poetry should embrace every part of our existence, the only acceptable test being whether or not the transformation of life's raw material into poetry had been accomplished successfully. *Hiraeth*, a hopeless longing for past friendships and remembered associations, did indeed run through all his work; but he was no mere escapist. According to Llywelyn-Williams the whole point of Gruffydd's most celebrated long poem, 'Ynys yr Hud' *(The Magic Island)*, is that the dozen young men who sailed away to look for wonders in distant lands had made a mistake: *the Lord's miracles* were to be found nearer home. And however scratchy Gruffydd's personality might have been, his sympathy with the ordinary unromantic *gwerin*, among whom he had been brought up, was profound: in his poetry he had created pictures of poverty-stricken, suffering individuals which even within their localized Welsh setting had *a supra-local significance*.

74

Yet a few years after the publication of Y Nos, Y
NIWL A'R YNYS we find Llywelyn-Williams telling
Bedwyr Lewis Jones that at the root of the
Romantic inspiration *there was a kind of lie, the lie of*
hiraeth, and going on to assert that *the myth of the*
Romantics was based on an appeal to the past or to a distant,
unreal, negative beauty. Then, damning Gruffydd by
implication, he says, *not one of them could create beauty*
out of the world and the life around them, and since there was
such an obvious gap between their daily lives and the vague
nostalgia that nourished their imagination it is no wonder
they ended up in a mood of disillusion and disgust. By the
time of his recorded conversation with Gwyn
Thomas his estimate of Gruffydd's poetic output
had become decidedly lukewarm.

However, the pendulum swung again. The
Cymmrodorion Lecture that Llywelyn-Williams
delivered in 1971 is a celebration of the Welsh
Romantic movement as represented by T. Gwynn
Jones—whom, in another context, he bracketed
with Dafydd ap Gwilym, Pantycelyn and Ann
Griffiths. And he makes a point not unlike the
one he had once made about Gruffydd when he
says that although Gwynn Jones created an ideal
world of the imagination he was not running
away from reality: his object was to inspire the
nation to action at a critical period.

Such oscillations in opinion, and the unracharac-
teristic violence of his off-the-cuff remarks, are
interesting. Llywelyn-Williams has told us of the
tensions in his mind between English and Welsh
and between poetry and history. But a third
tension (or perhaps a third manifestation of
some underlying conflict) seems to be present.

75

He clung to the idea that Welsh-language poetry should reflect the contemporary scene, and yet in his own work he constantly looks back. He must have known very well that his poetry is simply drenched with *hiraeth*. When he attacked Welsh Romanticism so vehemently was he lashing out at a troublesome part of himself? It is a possibility.

After settling down in Bangor he continued to write for the serious magazines. In 1970 half a dozen of these essays were collected into a volume, which appeared under the title NES NA'R HANESYDD? (*Nearer than the Historian?*). The query, incidentally, relates to the final couplet of a sonnet by Robert Williams-Parry, which declares that the historian does not come as close to the truth of 'what really happened' as the dramatist, who stands for the artistic imagination —a notion bound to fascinate a mind like that of Llywelyn-Williams. Sixteen or seventeen years later, when he was already a sick man, he chose eight further pieces for publication: most of them had been given as lectures. AMBELL SYLW (*Occasional Observations*) appeared posthumously, with a sensitive introduction by his friend and colleague Dyfnallt Morgan.

An essay in the earlier book deals, among other things, with the role of the literary critic. Saunders Lewis, we are told, believed that it was *to express his experience of the world*: literary criticism had to do with life in its fullness, with politics and religion, with the society that authors lived in. This is quite an apt description of the kind of criticism which Llywelyn-Williams him-

76

self began to turn out after the war, and which had little in common with the detailed analysis of texts then coming into fashion. On the whole he abstains from jargon and writes with what Arnold called largeness and benignity. His main aim is, in Dyfnallt Morgan's phrase, *to arouse new and intenser degrees of sensibility in his readers and himself.* The style is personal, semi-conversational and engaging—curiously reminiscent of that threatened species, the English 'man of letters'—and he is noticeably less combative than he used to be. Anyone who has no Welsh can capture the flavour by turning to the little book on R. T. Jenkins in this series, one of the few things the mature Llewelyn-Williams wrote in English.

The range of his reading is wide, of his subject-matter less so. Apart from some essays on poetic theory his literary criticism proper centres on comparatively recent work in Welsh. Names and topics tend to recur. But what he has to say is so common-sensible and wise—judicious might be a better word—that it never fails to hold the attention.

The creative writers whom he looks at individually are T. Gwynn Jones, Kate Roberts and Saunders Lewis. His observations on the novels and short stories of Kate Roberts were made in her presence, and were intended as a tribute, not an appraisal; but he provides some valuable insights into her very special talent. He discusses the long series of poems composed by Gwynn Jones during an unflaggingly productive life with fascinated respect. In the case of Saunders Lewis, Llywelyn-Williams points out the negative and the positive aspects of his veneration for the principle of aristocracy: it issued, we are told, in some coarse satire directed against the bulk of his compatriots but also in dazzling plays—especially SIWAN, unsurpassed in our literature as a study of lawful authority and its burdens, and of the relationship between passion and love.

Llywelyn-Williams was more than a purely literary critic, however. In an early lecture he tackled the fact, so embarrassing to broadcasters, that there was no standard spoken Welsh (except 'the language of the pulpit') and the related fact that Welsh in its written form was several centuries out of date. References to history and historiography abound. Building on what he had once written in Y LLENOR and TIR NEWYDD, he makes much of the comparison between two interpretations of Welsh history, the first that of the *gwerin* slowly freeing itself from feudal and other oppression, demanding to be educated, and finally entering into its inheritance; the second that of a Catholic, well-governed, independent, medieval Wales which disappeared, and to the ethos of which we should return as soon as possible. Llywelyn-Williams declares that both these influential theories are myths, but that one is infinitely more acceptable than the other.

Even when he deals with strictly literary subjects he almost always approaches them historically, and as one would expect he is particularly good at surveying important movements and placing them in their contexts, social, religious and political. In these surveys the interaction between aesthetic and historical judgements is notably

fruitful. Apart from Y Nos, Y NIWL A'R YNYS itself,
the outstanding instance is probably his account
of the Welsh-speaking poets of the First World
War, whose work had been much neglected.

His essays on *vers libre*, poetic language, the nature
of poetry and the social role of the poet draw, of
necessity, on the pronouncements of earlier
critics, but have a slant of their own. Most of his
ideas about the nature of poetry take their inspiration from Coleridge and Wordsworth. As
we have seen, Llywelyn-Williams believed that
the poet's fundamental aim was *to convey sensation*
or *to re-create in words a particular state of sensibility*, and
he made bold to assert that this aim lay *at the root
of every kind of poetry*. But the art also has a contemporary social significance: *every age ... demands
of the poet a new declaration of his individual experience.*
In our own confused era we can see the problems
but we cannot *perceive them with the imagination.* That
is where poets come in. Llywelyn-Williams, writing before he had begun to fear that science and
technology were getting out of control, renews
and deepens his youthful plea for their assimila-
tion into poetry. We need poets who will take
the new age of steel into their experience, and express, through the force of their imagination, *a
creative and integrating view.* But the poet has an even
greater responsibility. He *serves a mystery ... the
mystery of life itself ... It is the poet's privilege to testify to
the power of this mystery and to set it forth in words.* Or, as
Llywelyn-Williams put it in a couplet already
referred to,

*Life goes on, and God demands of the poet
A praise-song for the mystery and miracle of existence.*

(What he means by 'God' is another matter.) Going further, he writes in a collection of essays edited by Meic Stephens that though poetry *can't attempt any solutions to the eternal paradox of human life* it *can at least ... articulate our occasional glimpses of universal truth.*

How many contemporary poets would subscribe to such an exalted theory of their function and how well the theory would stand up to rigorous investigation are questions which we need not go into. What one cannot doubt is the essential nobility of the ideas he puts forward.

Llywelyn-Williams discussed the social role of poetry more specifically when he gave the Radio Wales Lecture for 1966 (it is reproduced in AMBELL SYLW). Here he is concerned with the position of poetry, and creative writing generally, in a bilingual country—or rather, as he carefully explains, in a country where a part of the population knows two languages, so that *every Welsh-speaking Welshman is a member of two societies, the one, as it were, being included in the other.* Llywelyn-Williams lists the difficulties with precision and sympathy. He insists that bilingual authors have the right to choose, on personal and artistic grounds, which language to work in, and he generously commends the productions of some who have chosen English. But he declares that the Welsh identity has always been bound up with the Welsh language, now in extreme danger, and that the author who chooses Welsh is directly helping to sustain a beleaguered community, as many a court poet must have done in the past.

Perhaps, after all, the chief justification for writing in Welsh . . . is that it's an expression of our self-respect as a society and of our determination to struggle against oblivion.

XII

At no stage was Alun Llywelyn-Williams a facile writer, but he liked few things more than putting words on paper. For the last nine or ten years of his life, however, he produced very little, and eventually he gave up writing altogether. The reason was simple, and sad: physical pain had become too much for him. The trouble appeared to be spinal, but the physicians and surgeons could never agree on a diagnosis. Laymen might remember his appalling war wounds and the accident in the inspection-pit; they might think of the condition that kept a little boy's hand in a splint for so long; they might imagine the jarring slips and falls of mountain-climbing; but these speculations were of no service to the doctors, who never succeeded in giving him more than temporary relief. I recall asking Alun, some time before he retired, how he was: he told me he was in pain every waking moment, and that he managed to sleep only with the aid of strong drugs *(the drugs of night and the reality of day)*.

Alun bore his suffering with a stoicism that was quite extraordinary. He preferred not to talk about what he was going through but his ravaged face was eloquent enough. His state became worse, and he died on 9 May 1988.

Various distinctions had come his way latterly. Bangor awarded him a personal Chair and after-wards the title of Professor Emeritus. The University made him a D.Litt. He was honoured by University College, Cardiff and by the Welsh Academy which he had helped to found. All this gave him pleasure. Friends often visited him, and when necessary some of them would run him to hospital. He found comfort in their goodwill and in the deep affection of his two daughters and their families. But everyone could see that it was the love, the cheerful, tireless devotion, and the nursing skills of his wife Alis which more than anything else sustained him during those last tormenting years.

Bibliography

ALUN LLYWELYN-WILLIAMS

Books and Monographs by Alun Llywelyn-Williams

CERDDI 1934–42, Foyle, London, 1944.

PONT Y CANIEDYDD, Gee, Denbigh, 1956.

CRWYDRO ARFON, Llyfrau'r Dryw, Llandybïe, 1959.

Y NOS, Y NIWL A'R YNYS, University of Wales Press, Cardiff, 1960.

Y LLENOR A'I GYMDEITHAS, BBC, London, 1966.

NES NA'R HANESYDD?, Gee, Denbigh, 1968.

GWANWYN YN Y DDINAS, Gee, Denbigh, 1975.

R. T. JENKINS, University of Wales Press on behalf of the Welsh Arts Council, Cardiff, 1977.

Y GOLAU YN Y GWYLL, Gee, Denbigh, 1979.

AMBELL SYLW (published posthumously), Gee, Denbigh, 1988.

Some Articles and Interviews

'Barddoniaeth mewn oes ddiwydiannol', in Y LLENOR, Spring 1935.

'W. J. Gruffydd', in GWŶR LLÊN, ed. Aneirin Talfan Davies, Griffiths, London, 1948.

Llywelyn-Williams contributed an account of his own work to ARTISTS IN WALES, 2, ed. Meic Stephens, Gomer, Llandysul, 1973.

Transcripts of interviews which he gave were published in YSGRIFAU BEIRNIADOL I, ed. J. E. Caerwyn Williams, Gee, Denbigh, 1965, MABON, 4, 1971, and LLAIS LLYFRAU, Winter 1986. The interviewers were (i) Bedwyr Lewis Jones, (ii) and (iii) Gwyn Thomas.

Edited by Alun Llywelyn-Williams

TIR NEWYDD (quarterly, 1935–9). Published privately at first, then from October 1936 by Gwasg y Brython, Liverpool.

Some Appreciations

Geraint Bowen, 'Cerddi Alun Llywelyn-Williams', in Y LLENOR, Spring 1949.

Dafydd Glyn Jones, 'The Poetry of Alun Llywelyn-Williams', in *Poetry Wales*, 7, no. 1, 1971.

Glyn Jones and John Rowlands in PROFILES, Gomer, Llandysul, 1980.

Gwyn Thomas and Wynford Vaughan-Thomas, in BARN, February 1984. The issue also contains a poem on Llywelyn-Williams by Alan Llwyd.

Gwyn Thomas, ALUN LLYWELYN-WILLIAMS, Gwasg Pantycelyn, Caernarfon, 1987.

D. Llewelyn Walters, in Y FANER, 3 June 1988.

Dyfnallt Morgan in TALIESIN, July 1988. The issue also contains a memorial poem by R. Gerallt Jones.

Rhydwen Williams in BARDDAS, July 1988.

Bedwyr Lewis Jones, Elwyn Evans, Alun Oldfield-Davies, R. Geraint Gruffydd and Gwyn Thomas in BARN, August 1988. (A transcript of the radio programme produced by R. Alun Evans and broadcast on 15 May.)

Dyfnallt Morgan, introduction to AMBELL SYLW, Gee, Denbigh, 1988.

The Welsh Academy held a memorial meeting for Alun Llywelyn-Williams at Bangor on 24 September 1988. The proceedings were recorded, and tapes of the addresses by R. Gerallt Jones and Dyfnallt Morgan are held in the Academy's archives.

Acknowledgements

Grateful thanks are due to Mrs Alis Llywelyn-Williams for supplying valuable information, to Mr Dyfnallt Morgan and Dr Glyn Jones for their kindness in reading and commenting on a draft of this essay, and to Mrs Luned Meredith, Mrs Non Jenkins, Mrs Sara Dobson and the staffs of the Welsh Academy and the London Library for various forms of practical help.

Translations of passages from GWANWYN YN Y DDINAS and Y GOLAU YN Y GWYLL appear by permission of Mrs Llywelyn-Williams and from NES NA'R HANESYDD? and YSGRIFAU BEIRNIADOL by permission of Gwasg Gee. The translations are by Elwyn Evans.

The Author

Elwyn Evans, son of the poet Wil Ifan, was born in 1912 and educated at Cardiff, Bridgend and Oxford. He joined the BBC as an announcer, becoming a producer when the Welsh Region was formed. During the Second World War he served for four years in the Middle East, an experience reflected in his own poems. As a features producer in the fifties he brought much Welsh material into the Home Service and the Third Programme. In 1956 he was seconded to West Africa as Director of Programmes of the newly established Nigerian Broadcasting Corporation: with his wife and daughter he lived in Nigeria for three years. On his return to Britain he became Head of the BBC's Radio Training Section in London, retiring in 1972. He has published two collections of Welsh verse and, in English, a book on the art of radio.

This Edition,
designed by Jeff Clements,
is set in Monotype Spectrum 12 Didot on 13 point
and printed on Basingwerk Parchment by
Qualitex Printing Limited, Cardiff

It is limited to 1000 copies of which this is

Copy No. 0324

British Library Cataloguing in Publication Data

Evans, Elwyn 1912–
   Alun Llywelyn-Williams. — (Writers of Wales; 0141-5050).
   1. Welsh poetry
   I. Title   II. Series
   891.6612

ISBN 0-7083-1103-2